7 Bites Series Bariatric Cookbook Seasons 1-3

Jennifer DeMoss
Suzette Munson

Copyright © 2015

7 Bites Show

All Rights Reserved

Also from Jennifer DeMoss and Suzette Munson

Breaking the Chains: A Guide To Bariatric Surgery

This book is dedicated with love and devotion to our Friends on the web, to our amazing families, and to our Lord and Savior Jesus Christ, with whom this book would not have happened.

Welcome to our very first cookbook! We are so excited to share these recipes and stories with you – some of which weren't available before now! We hope that you'll be able to use these recipes to your advantage and that our stories amuse, inspire, and encourage you. We encourage you to take these recipes and make them your own! Switch up ingredients, change up proteins, add or remove spices. Remember these recipes are more about learning a method than anything else. Remember the old saying, "give a man a fish, feed him for a day. Teach a man to fish, feed him for a lifetime!" We want to be the ones to teach you to fish!

Who are we?

Jen and Sue are both bariatric patients. Suzette had gastric band in 2003, and had a revision to the gastric sleeve in 2012. Jennifer had gastric sleeve in 2012. Together we have lost (and maintained a loss) of over 255 lbs.! We did it by maintaining bariatric eating guidelines including high protein foods in smaller portions, but also remembered that even a bariatric patient has to live a life without obsessing over every bite of food we eat. We started our cooking series 7 Bites in 2013 after realizing how little information there was at that time for post-op patients. We are one of the first bariatric cooking series ever, and the first 100% web-based bariatric cooking series on YouTube. We love to visit with bariatric support groups and love to discuss all aspects of the surgery from start to finish. Our goal is to help and get information out to as many people out there that need it as possible!

About our recipes:

We have a philosophy around our eating – eat healthy 95% of the time. 5% of the time is reserved for the occasional treat. To that end, we DO have some recipes that aren't low carb, we DO have some recipes that aren't sugar-free, and we DO have some recipes that aren't low fat. That being said, the majority of our recipes are low-carb and/or high-protein.

Most of our recipes are as whole and natural as possible. We believe in real food as opposed to pre-packaged and/or boxed foods. Where we do use sweeteners, we try to offer alternative ingredients to those that are sensitive to that type of thing. We don't believe in fad diets, and we don't rely on using a lot of pre-packaged foods (although we have been known to sneak a cake mix in occasionally!).

We also try to focus on foods that the entire family can enjoy. Since Suzette is a grandmother and Jennifer is a mom (of four!!) making sure that the family is involved in healthy eating is important. That being said, we also understand that there are a lot of people out there who are single or with smaller families, so we have recipes that are for one or two servings as well!

Our recipes vary from phase to phase, so you will be certain to find one for you whatever your diet phase may be.

Why we don't list nutrition information:

This is a hot topic for us and our viewers. We don't offer nutrition information for a very specific purpose – different ingredients can vary in nutritional information depending on what brand of said ingredient is used. For example, three protein powders that we have used have a different amount of calories, protein, and sodium. The same recipe made using these different powders differ in protein by 5-15 grams! So we encourage you to use the tools available to you to find nutrition information through web sites and recipe builders you can find online. If we were able to list the specific brands we use, then we would be able to have specific nutrition information. Sadly, legally we can't do that right now (maybe in the future we'll have lots of culinary sponsors!).

How to contact us:

We love to connect with our friends! You can reach us via email sevenbitesshow@gmail.com on Facebook www.facebook.com/7Bites on our Facebook group www.facebook.com/groups/7Bites or on our website www.7Bites.net We will answer any question you might have!

Abbreviations:

C – Cup
T/Tbsp. – Tablespoon
t/tsp. – Teaspoon
lb. – Pound
oz. – Ounce
pt. – Pint
qt. – Quart
ml/mL – Milliliter
L – Liter
g – gram
Kg - Kilogram

Measurements and Substitutions

Weight

US	½ oz.	1 oz.	4 oz. (1/4 lb.)	8 oz. (1/2 lb.)	16 oz. (1 lb.)	1 ¼ lb.	1 ½ lb.	2 lb.
Metric	15 g	25/30 g	115-125 g	225-250 g	450-500 g	625 g	750 g	1,000 g 1 Kg

Temperature

300 F	325 F	350 F	375 F	400 F	425 F	450 F	475 F	500 F	Broil
150C	160C	180C	190C	200C	220C	230C	240C	260C	Broil

Liquid Measurement

US = Standard Metric
1/8 tsp = 0.5 mL
¼ tsp = 1 mL
½ tsp = 2 mL
1 tsp = 5 mL
1 T = 15 mL
2 T = 25 mL
¼ C = 2 fl. oz. = 50 mL
1/3 C = 3 fl. oz. = 75 mL
½ C = 4 fl. oz. = 125 mL
2/3 C = 5 fl. oz. = 150 mL
¾ C = 6 fl. oz. = 175 mL
1 C = 8 fl. oz. = 250 mL
2 C = 1 pt. = 500 mL
1 qts = 1 L

Weights and Measures

3 tsp = 1 T
4 T = ¼ C
5 1/3 T = 1/3 C
8 T = ½ C
10 2/3 T = 2/3 C
12 T = ¾ C
16 T = 1 C

Measure	Equivalent Measure	Equivalent Oz
1 T		½ fl. oz.
1 C	½ pt.	8 fl. oz.
2 C	1 pt.	16 fl. oz.
2 pts (4 C)	1 qts	32 fl. oz.
4 qts (16 C)	1 gallon	128 fl. oz.

Bariatric Serving Sizes

Remember that the amount you're actually able to eat may differ from what is shown here. Try to avoid high-fat foods and "slider" foods (foods that go down easy and you can eat a lot of such as crackers, popcorn, potato chips, etc.) Also be sure to add about 1 T of healthy fats daily!

Protein:

2-3 oz. cooked meat or fish
½ C tofu
¼ C beans or lentils

Dairy:

1 whole egg or 1 egg white or ¼ C egg substitute
½ -1 C yogurt
1 C milk or milk alternative
1 oz. cheese
¼ C cottage cheese
1 string cheese or round cheese snack (the ones in the red wax with the cute cow on them *wink*)

Vegetables:

1 C salad greens
¼-1/2 C cooked vegetables
¼-1/2 chopped raw veggies

Starches:

½ C potatoes or ½ small potato
¼ C corn or ½ ear corn on cob or peas
2 T rice, quinoa, or other grain
1 slice whole-grain bread or 1 small whole-grain tortilla
5 whole grain crackers

Season 1

Season 1 was so much fun for us. It was not only our first time to be in front of a camera, but it was our film crew's first time at filming a show. Not only that, but we had "outsiders" with us while we were filming a few episodes (Jen's sister Aimee and niece Heather were helpers). So there was some distraction going on – along with a learning curve!

Jen recalls, "It was SO nerve-wracking. I kept looking at my sister, who was standing off camera. Also, I couldn't see my husband (sound engineer and director, Ronnie DeMoss) so I had NO idea when he was giving me a signal. Looking back on it, it could have ended up a total train-wreck! Thankfully, it didn't and the episodes all turned out pretty good!" Jen's favorite episode from this season is "Halloween Nutz": "My mom and I had the BEST time filming our alternate personas. We are huge fans of Ree Drummand (The Pioneer Woman) and Paula Deen. So when we were talking about costumes, those seemed like the most natural choices for us! We giggled a lot during filming." Her favorite recipe from this season is, "All of them! No, really, they're all amazing recipes and I actually use most of them on a regular basis!"

Sue remembers that she was, "scared to death, having to see myself on camera and listen to myself talk! I know I talk slow, but boy did my 'Texas' show itself!" She wanted to make sure that the important information every bariatric patient needed was easily available because, "I wanted to make sure that others did no have to go throught he pain and agony of trial and error. I know there will be alot of that anyway, but I felt we could make it easier for those coming behind us." Sue loved having her grandaughter Heather on the set for "Decadant Desserts (That Aren't)", but her favorite episodes are the recipe makeovers. "I'd find a great recipe and lighten up and also added protein elements that hadn't been added before," resulting in great food that was not only delicious, but bariatric-friendly.

From *Something For Everyone*

Meatloaf Bites

This recipe has become a staple in our diets. We mix it up a lot and have made so many variations on this recipe! We encourage you to take it and make it your own!

Yield:
24 bites - about 12 bariatric servings

1 lb. lean ground beef
1 egg, beaten
Glaze:
½ C ketchup
1 T favorite steak sauce

Combine glaze mix in a bowl and set aside.
In a separate bowl combine meat, egg, and ½ the glaze. Mix well with your hands. Divide by the Tablespoon to mini muffin tins sprayed with cooking spray (about 2 T per tin). Top each bite with about a teaspoon of glaze.
Bake at 425 for 15-20 minutes or until internal temperature reads 155-160. Allow to set for 5-10 minutes before serving.

From Cauliflower Power

Jen's Cauli-Tatos

Jen's oldest prides himself on the fact that he's so picky about what he eats. He's a pizza/French fries/fast food kinda guy, so when he asked for these BY NAME ... Well, let's just say that if HE likes it, there's a good chance YOUR family will like it!

16 Bariatric Servings (1/4 C)

1 head of cauliflower cut into florets and washed
2 red potatoes, washed and cut into 1-1/2 inch pieces (you want them close to the same size as the cauliflower)

Cover the veggies with chicken stock and add about a teaspoon or so of salt. Bring to a boil over medium high heat, then reduce the heat and boil until potatoes and cauliflower are fork tender. Drain.

Making the Cauli-Tatos

While the potatoes and cauliflower are draining in a strainer, add to your pan:
2 T Butter, softened
1/2 block of cream cheese, softened
1/4 C milk
salt and pepper to taste

Heat these ingredients until the butter melts. Add the cauliflower and the potatoes back into the pan and mash slightly. Using an immersion blender if you have it, blend everything together until almost smooth. If you don't have an immersion blender, toss it into the food processor and process until almost smooth. If you don't want chunks, process until completely smooth. Transfer mixture to a greased 9X9 baking pan. Bake at 350 degrees for 15-20 minutes until hot and browned on top.

**For single-serving portions that are equal to 2 tablespoons, add two beaten eggs before processing and spoon into mini-muffin tins. These will bake at 350 degrees for about 5-7 minutes. Keep an eye on them to prevent over browning, and allow them to sit and cool for at least 10 minutes so they hold their shape*

Sue's Cauli Mac and Cheese

The very best part of this is the sauce. If you are on full solids or purees, try making the sauce and eating it on its own! It's wonderful, delicious, and "Soooo silky!"

16 Bariatric Servings (1/4 C)

1 head cauliflower, cut into florets
1 1/2 C heavy cream
4 oz. cream cheese
2 C shredded cheese of choice
3 tsp. brown mustard
1/8 tsp. garlic powder
1/4 tsp. salt
1/4 tsp. pepper
1/4 tsp. cayenne

Cover cauliflower with chicken stock and add about a teaspoon of salt. Bring to a boil over medium high heat, then reduce the heat to medium and continue to boil until fork tender. Drain completely. Add remaining ingredients to a medium sauce pan and heat over medium heat stirring constantly until smooth. Add to cooked cauliflower and mix well, then turn out into a greased 9X9 pan. Top with another 1/2 C cheese. Bake at 350 15-20 minutes or until hot, bubbly, and brown.

From Halloween Nutz

Cajun Spiced Nuts

Proof that we're a bit spicy ... and a bit nutty! These are great to have on hand if you have a love of things that are salty and crunchy.

16 Bariatric Servings (1/4 C each)

2 large egg whites
2 tsp. water
½ tsp. sea salt
½ tsp. garlic powder
½ tsp. chili powder
½ tsp. ground cumin
¼ tsp. cayenne pepper

4 cups assorted nuts (we used almonds, cashews, peanuts, and pecans)

Beat egg whites until frothy and add water and seasonings. Beat until combined. Pour nuts into a large plastic bag. Pour mixture over the nuts and massage until well coated. If desired, allow them to sit for an hour. Turn out on baking sheet lined with silicone mat or parchment paper (or well oiled baking sheet). Bake at 325 for 20-25 minutes. Cool on pan. Store in an air tight container for up to a week.

Roasted Honey Nuts

If you have a sweet tooth, these are awesome. Try adding some cinnamon for a delicious treat!

8 Bariatric Servings (1/4 C)
1 T honey
1 T vegetable oil
1 T water
2 C nuts of choice (we used almonds)
2 T sweetener of choice (we like sucralose or stevia)

Combine honey, water, and vegetable oil in a bowl and pour into plastic bag. Add nuts and massage until well coated. Add sweetener and toss until coated. Allow to sit for a few minutes then turn out onto a silicone mat or parchment lined baking sheet. Bake at 325 for 20-25 minutes. Cool on pan. Store in an air tight container for up to a week.

Pecan Bites

Oh, the decadence!! You SERIOUSLY only need one, these are so rich! The agave syrup will add carbs and sugars to the recipe, but it has a lower glycemic index, so it shouldn't cause dumping like corn syrup would.

24 Bariatric Servings (24 1 in squares)

2 C almond flour
1 stick cold butter, cut into bits
2 C agave syrup
1 C sugar substitute
6 eggs
2 tsp. vanilla
2 C chopped pecans

Crust: Add almond flour and butter to food processor and pulse until well combined. Turn out into 9X13 pan well prepared with cooking spray, butter, or oil of choice.

Filling: Pour pecans into crust. Combine other ingredients in a large bowl and pour over pecans. Bake 325 about 40-45 minutes or until set.

From Decadent Desserts (That Aren't)

Filo Pudding Cups

Heather still loves these. We can't blame her. They're awesome. And she was an awesome helper!

Number of servings depends on how many filo cups you have.
1 filo cup= 1 serving

Sugar Free Pudding Mix, prepared according to package directions
Pre-made filo dough cups OR filo dough (cups recipe follows)
Sugar Free whipped topping
Sugar free toppings such s caramel or chocolate

Filo Dough Cups:
Lay a sheet of filo dough on a clean counter or tea towel. Lightly spray with cooking spray. Top with another sheet of filo dough and repeat. Repeat with 3-4 sheets. Using a cookie cutter, cut the sheets into rounds and tuck into a muffin tin. Bake at 350 for 15-20 minutes or until slightly browned.

Fill with a spoon full or two of pudding and top with sugar free toppings of choice.

From Fall Favorites

Jen's Fun Chili

Sue still doesn't "get" the addition of sweetener and cinnamon. That's okay. She doesn't have to. This chili still rocks.

24 bariatric servings (about ½ C each)

2 lbs. lean ground beef
1 medium onion, chopped
2 cloves garlic, minced
1 6 oz. can tomato paste
1 28 can crushed tomatoes
12 oz. good craft beer
1/4 C Chili powder
1 tsp. ground black pepper
2 tsp. salt, cumin, paprika, garlic powder, onion powder, oregano
1/2 tsp. red pepper flake (or to taste)
1 T brown sugar substitute
2 tsp. cinnamon

Stovetop directions:
Brown ground beef with onions and garlic until no longer pink and onions are tender. Add all remaining ingredients and mix well. Bring to a bubble over medium high heat, then turn to medium low and simmer for up to 2 1/2 hours, stirring occasionally. If it looks like the liquid is evaporating too quickly, add some broth or more beer (water will dilute the flavor!).

Slow cooker directions:

Brown ground beef with onions and garlic until no longer pink and onions are tender. Combine remaining ingredients in slow cooker and mix well to combine. Add meat mixture and stir well to combine. Cook on low up to 12 hours or on high up to 8 hours. If it looks like it needs more liquid after a few hours, add more beer or add some beef broth (water will dilute the flavor!)

Mom's Beef Stew

This is a classic dish that everyone needs in their repertoire. The tomato paste thickens the stew so that you don't need additional flour. PS - this recipe can be pureed beautifully and is absolutely delicious when you're on the pureed stage!

2 lbs. stew meat dredged in 1/2 C soy flour and seasoned with salt and pepper to taste
2 T oil
1 box beef broth
2 T tomato paste
2 medium red potatoes, peeled if desired and cut into bite size pieces
1/2 medium bag baby carrots
1/2 large onion, chopped
1 clove garlic
2 sprigs fresh rosemary
2 T "road kill seasoning" (garlic powder, salt and pepper)
1 C wine (red or white works!)

Stove top:
Brown dredged and seasoned stew meat in oil in large stock pot. De-glaze pan using 1 C beef broth. Add tomato paste and mix well. Add remaining broth and wine and stir well to combine. Add remaining ingredients and stir. Bring to a boil over medium high heat then reduce heat to medium low. Simmer for up to 2 hours,

stirring occasionally. Add more broth if it looks as though the liquid is evaporating too quickly.

Slow Cooker:
Brown dredged and seasoned stew meat in oil. De-glaze pan with 1 C beef broth. Transfer to slow cooker and add remaining ingredients. Stir well to combine. Cook on low for up to 12 hours or on high for up to 8 hours. If it looks like the liquid is evaporating too quickly after a couple of hours, add more broth.

Variations:
	*Add a handful of greens to the stew during the last 15-20 minutes for a great veggie boost!
	* Use whatever veggies you have on hand! Green beans, scallions, turnips, sweet potatoes…
		Any hardy vegetable works great!

From <u>Happy Thanksgiving from 7 Bites</u>

Whole Turkey Breast

Besides the drumsticks, the breast is the only part of the turkey our family eats! So instead of investing in a large turkey, we bought the part that everyone likes! The amount of butter we used SEEMS like a lot, but it actually comes down to about 1 serving of butter (1/2 T) per 3 oz. serving. But if you feel like you HAVE to omit it, feel free to use olive, coconut, or another oil of choice instead.

16 bariatric servings (about 3 oz. each)

1 Whole Turkey Breast (3 lb.)
1 stick butter, softened
1/4 C chopped fresh herbs (we used rosemary, thyme, and chives!)
Couple of teaspoons dried marjoram and/or savory

Wash turkey breast and pat dry. Set in roasting pan.
Combine softened butter with herbs. Slather on turkey skin. Using your finger, gently separate the skin from the meat slightly and add more herb butter under the skin.
Cover the bird with foil and roast at 325 for 2 hours, remove foil and finish cooking 30 minutes or until meat thermometer reads 155-160. Allow to rest for at least 10 minutes before carving - this will allow any carry-over cooking to finish and for the meats juices to redistribute.

Glazes

Orange Glaze option
1 C orange juice
1 C orange marmalade
2 T orange liqueur

Apricot Glaze option
1 C apricot nectar
1 C apricot jam
2 T Amaretto liqueur

Combine all ingredients in a saucepan and heat over medium-low heat, stirring often, until reduced by half and thickened. Serve warm alongside meat of choice.

The Dressing

Carbs are no longer a staple in our diet, but we do make allowances for holidays! This dressing is made from all cornbread – no biscuits or bread added!

About 24 Bariatric Servings (1 dressing muffin or 2 dressing mini-muffins per serving)

1 recipe Cornbread
1 onion, chopped
1 rib celery, chopped
1/2 C chopped pecans
1 T fresh rosemary
1 tsp. of the following: Dried parsley, marjoram, thyme (you can add sage if you like it. We don't because Mom's allergic to it!!)
salt and pepper to taste
1 egg
1 C chicken broth

Cornbread:

1 C cornmeal
1 C flour
2 tsp. baking powder
1 tsp. salt
1 T sugar substitute (optional)
1 T melted butter
1 egg
3/4 C milk

Combine dry ingredients in large bowl. Whisk wet ingredients in smaller bowl. Add wet ingredients to dry ingredients and mix until well blended. Pour into sheet pan. Bake at 350 for 15-20 minutes or until toothpick comes out clean.
NOTE You can make this gluten free by substituting 1 C gluten-free baking mix for the flour OR by using all cornmeal!

The Dressing
Cut cornbread into cubes and allow cornbread cubes to sit out overnight to dry OR dry in a 250 degree oven for about 2 hours. Sauté onions and celery 1 T olive oil plus 1 T butter. Add to a large bowl with cornbread cubes and toss gently to combine. Add pecans and herbs and toss to combine. Add egg and chicken broth and stir gently to combine

Use a spoon to fill some greased mini muffin tins...
You can also use individual-sized ramekins OR you can pour it into a 9X9 baking dish...

Bake them at 350 degrees:

Mini nuggets: 10-15 minutes
Individual ramekins: 20-25 minutes
9X9 baking dish: 30-35 minutes

Allow to cool for about 5 minutes before serving!
From *Thanksgiving Sides*

Green Bean Casserole

This is a wonderful recipe for those that love fresh green beans. We omitted the traditional cream soups and thickened it using arrowroot – a low-carb thickening agent. We also added fresh mushrooms and some vitamin-rich onions and bell peppers. This is a fresh twist on an old classic!

8-16 bariatric servings (1/4 C – ½ C)

1 lb. fresh green beans, washed, trimmed, and cut into bite-size pieces (about 1-1 1/2 in pieces)
1 onion, chopped
1 bell pepper, chopped (any color you like - we used red!)
1 package sliced mushrooms
2 T arrowroot
2 C chicken broth
1/2 C fried onions (optional)

Cut the green beans into smaller pieces (if you can't find fresh green beans, use frozen just thaw them first. In a REAL pinch, or if you don't like fresh green beans you can use two cans of green beans - just drain them first!).

Sauté the onions, peppers, and mushrooms in some olive oil and butter (if you want to, add about 2 minced garlic cloves!).
Add the green beans to the pan and toss. Add the broth and mix well. Combine it with about 2 T arrowroot with ¼ C broth to make

a slurry. Add the slurry to the pan and stir well. Bring up to a boil then stir gently until thickened. Pour into a greased casserole dish.

Bake at 350 for about 20-25 minutes. If desired, top with French fried onions the last 5 minutes of cooking!

The Sweet Potatoes

To our family, Thanksgiving is just not Thanksgiving without the sweet potatoes. Sweet potatoes are a great bariatric staple – they're full of iron, beta carotene and fiber!

6-8 bariatric servings (about ¼ C)

3-4 small-medium sweet potatoes, peeled, cut into 1-1 1/2 in pieces, and boiled until just fork tender
1/2 C brown sugar substitute (or more, if you want it!)
2 T molasses (optional)
2 T cinnamon (or more, if you want it!)
1/2 stick butter, softened

Place sweet potatoes into a greased baking dish or casserole dish. Add brown sugar and cinnamon. Drizzle with molasses if desired. Dot with butter. Bake at 350 for 30 minutes and stir. Continue to bake for another 15-20 minutes

From *Holiday Brunch*

Mimosas

Please note that we do not condone drinking alcohol or carbonation on a regular basis, if at all. This is a SPECIAL drink recipe. The champagne can be completely omitted and replaced with sparkling cider, ginger ale, or lemon-lime soda. The orange juice breaks the carbonation.

6-12 Bariatric Servings (1/4-1/2 C)
Ingredients:

For the adults:

2 Orange juice (we used a low-acid variety, but you can use whichever one you like and tolerate best!) - more if needed!
1 bottle champagne (we used a Brut [dry])

For the kids:

2 C Orange Juice
4 C ginger ale, seltzer, or lemon-lime soda

Pour juice into a 2 qt. pitcher. Add champagne and stir gently to combine. If needed, add more juice to taste. Pour into wine glasses or champagne flutes and enjoy!

TIP for a festive presentation, garnish the glass with a strawberry or float a maraschino cherry on the bottom (my daughter's favorite!)

Sausage Balls

This recipe is super easy. If you're totally low-carbing, you can omit the baking mix completely and it will still work!

12 Bariatric Servings (24 Balls – 2 Balls/serving)

1-1 lb. roll breakfast sausage (look for one with no MSG!)
2 C shredded cheese (we used smoked Gouda for a special change!)
1 C baking mix (ours was a gluten-free variety)
1/4 C water

Combine all ingredients in a bowl with your hands until well combined. Using a small ice-cream or cookie scoop, shape into balls and place on baking sheet lined with parchment paper. Bake at 425 for 15-20 minutes or until browned and sizzling. Place on paper towels to drain off before serving - these are great hot out of the oven or room temperature!!
These nuggets are chock full of protein
and flavor and are a kid-pleaser!

Egg Cups

This is a staple!! It can be tweaked and changed to fit your taste. Use whatever cheese, meat, or veggies you like!

12 Bariatric Servings (1 Egg cup per serving)

8 eggs
1/2 C heavy cream
1 1/2 C shredded cheese (we used Jarlsburg Swiss for this - but you can use whichever cheese is your favorite!)
4 slices cooked bacon, chopped or crumbled

Combine eggs and cream in a large bowl with whisk until well blended. Divide cheese and bacon evenly into 12 greased muffin tins (liners won't work for this - the egg will stick horribly to them!) Add egg mixture 1/4 C at a time until it is all used (it will divide evenly). Bake at 350 about 15 minutes or until puffy and browned slightly. They will deflate when you take them out of the oven so don't freak out! It's normal!! Remove from tins and allow to cool for a couple of minutes before eating.

From <u>Holiday Treats</u>

Stove Top Cookies

24 bariatric servings (1 cookie per serving)

1/2 C Milk
1 1/2 C Sugar Substitute
3 generous T cocoa
1 C chopped pecans
2 C flaked coconut (unsweetened)
1/2 C Crunch Peanut Butter
1 tsp. vanilla

Combine milk, sugar substitute and cocoa in a medium saucepan. Bring to a boil over medium heat, stirring consistently to prevent scalding. When steaming and starting to bubble along the sides of the pan, add remaining ingredients. Stir together until well combined.

Using a cookie scoop or spoon, spoon out onto lined baking sheet or plate and allow to cool for about 5-10 minutes before eating.

**Option: If you like it and are using carbs, use oatmeal in place of the coconut or substitute 1 cup of the coconut for the oatmeal! You can also use dried fruits in for added flavor and fiber!*

Stuffed Chocolate Dipped Strawberries

Amount of servings varies with amount of berries in the pint.
1 Strawberry = 1 Serving

1 Bag sugar free chocolate chips
1 pint strawberries, washed
1 block softened cream cheese
1/3 C sugar substitute
1 tsp. vanilla

In a bowl, combine softened cream cheese, sugar substitute and vanilla. Set aside.

Create a double boiler by setting a bowl over a saucepan with 1/2 in water in the bottom. Bring water to a boil, turn down to medium low and allow to gently simmer. Put chocolate chips in bowl and melt slowly, stirring often.

Hull the strawberries and cut a well into the stem area of each one. (If desired, stem and hull half the berries and leave the other half for just plain dipping!)

Fill the hole with a small spoonful of cream cheese mix (about 1/2 tsp). Dip the berries cream cheese side down to seal. If desired, cover the entire berry with chocolate!

Easy Overnight Meringues

12 Bariatric Servings (1 meringue per serving)

3 egg whites, room temperature
8 T Sugar Substitute

Beat egg whites until stiff peaks form. Spoon or pipe onto cookie sheet lined with parchment paper. Bake at 200 for 2 hours then turn off oven and allow to go for at least 8 hours (we do these overnight!). Garnish with leftover melted chocolate, dried fruit, berries - whatever you like!!

Option: add some flavor and color to them by adding 1 tsp vanilla, freeze dried fruits, cocoa powder, or other flavor extracts. Make sure if you're adding fruit that you fold it in gently after the peaks form!

From *Merry Christmas from 7 Bites*
Bacon-Wrapped Asparagus

Number of servings depends on amount of asparagus in package.
Note that you might not use all the bacon in the package
2 bundles = 1 serving

1 lb. asparagus, trimmed
1 lb. bacon
Cut bacon strips in half.
Bundle 3-4 trimmed asparagus spears together and wrap with bacon strip. Lay on a baking pan coated with cooking spray. Bake at 425 for 15-20 minutes or until bacon is crisp and asparagus is tender.

Lamb Chops

About 10-12 3 oz. servings (one chop per Bariatric Serving)

2 lbs. lean lamb chops
2 cups soy flour or other flour alternative (like almond meal, coconut flour, etc.)
Salt and pepper to taste

Heat ¼ C coconut oil in a pan over medium heat until reaches a temp of around 350. Sprinkle chops with salt and pepper and dredge lightly in soy flour. Fry in oil for 2-3 minutes per side, until well browned and transfer them to a baking sheet.

Transfer to a 225 oven for 25-30 minutes to gently finish cooking.

Roasted Garlic Mashed Potatoes

16 Bariatric Servings (1/4 C per serving)

2 heads garlic, tops trimmed off
2 T olive oil
2 tsp. salt
2 tsp. black pepper
1 recipe prepared mashed potatoes or mashed cauliflower (4 Cups)

Place one head of trimmed garlic on top of a piece of foil and top with oil, and one tsp each salt and pepper. Wrap tightly. Repeat with second garlic head. Pop them into a 425 oven for about 30 minutes or until you are able to really smell the garlic roasting. Remove them and allow them to cool.
Squeeze the roasted garlic bulbs into a bowl and mash with a fork. Transfer to potatoes and mix well.
Garnish with chopped chives, if desired.

From <u>New Year's Entertaining</u>

Stuffed Mushrooms

Amount of servings depends on how many mushrooms are in the package.
1 mushroom = 1 serving

1 package button or crimini mushrooms
½ lb. mild Italian sausage
½ C parmesan cheese
¼ C chopped parsley

Clean the mushrooms and pop the stems out. If desired, chop the stems for the filling. Place the sausage, cheese, and parsley in a bowl and mix well to combine. Divide mixture evenly between the mushrooms. Bake in a 350 oven for 20-25 minutes or until sausage is cooked through and mushrooms are tender. Allow to rest for at least 5 minutes before eating.

Mini Cheese Truffles

10-12 Bariatric Servings (1 Truffle per serving)

1 brick cream cheese with Greek yogurt, softened
1 lb. shredded cheese of choice (we used a sharp cheddar)
½ C chopped pecans
½ finely chopped parsley or other herbs

In a food processor, combine cream cheese and shredded cheese. Turn out into a bowl and chill for about an hour to firm up. Use a cookie scoop to scoop out about 2 T cheese mixture. Roll in between your hands to form a ball. Roll in chopped nuts or parsley gently pressing down to make the coating stick. Serve chilled.

Bacon-Wrapped Barbecue Mini Sausages

Number of servings depends on how many mini-sausages are in the package. 2 sausages = 1 serving

1 package mini smoked sausage
6-8 slices bacon, cut into quarters
1 bottle favorite barbecue sauce
1 can diet root beer

Wrap mini sausage with ¼ slice bacon and secure with a toothpick. Repeat with remaining sausages. Transfer to a slow cooker. Cook on low 2-3 hours.

Combine barbecue sauce and root beer in a small sauce pan. Bring to a boil and reduce heat to medium low. Simmer for 10-15 minutes, stirring often to reduce. Pour over sausages and cook for another 2-3 hours on low.

How to Cook and Eat an Artichoke in 10 Easy Steps

Step 1: Trim the pointed edges off the tops of the artichoke.
Step 2: If desired, peel the stem of the artichoke.
Step 3: Bring a large pot of water to a rapid boil
Step 4: Add artichokes and 1 lemon, halved.
Step 5: Boil 20-25 minutes or until artichoke is tender (a fork will pierce the stem easily)
Step 7: Remove from the water and allow to cool completely.
Step 8: Reach into the center of the artichoke and remove the choke (the fibrous portion on top of the heart.
Step 9: Eat the leaves – remove a leaf from the artichoke and use your teeth to scrape the meat from the bottom of the leaf
Step 10: Cut up the heart and stem and eat those.

Artichoke Dipping Sauce
½ C light mayonnaise or plain Greek yogurt
2 T lemon juice
Salt and pepper to taste

Stir all ingredients gently together. Serve with artichokes for dipping.

Stuffed Mini Tomatoes and Kalamata Olives

Servings vary. 1 olive or 1 tomato per serving.

Cut a slit into a cherry or grape tomato and stuff with a small pinch of blue cheese.

Stuff a little sliver of sharp cheddar into the hole of a pitted Kalamata olive

Season 2

During season 2, we started getting more comfortable in front of the camera, and the film crew started getting more creative with their shots. There was an ongoing theme of this season of cooking for holidays and entertaining.

Jen remembers, "I started getting getting better at cutting recipes down. I'd been used to cooking HUGE meals for my family and me, but after surgery, we started eating less and less. So rather than cooking huge pots of soup, crock pots full of chili, or giant casseroles, I was making more individual-sized meals and portions. It was a lot of fun for me to experiment and come into my own as a cook." One of her favorite dishes this season was the shrimp kabobs from "Be My Valentine". "Valentine's Day is one of my favorite holidays anyway, and that shrimp kabob was so stinking cute! I was so proud of that," she laughs. Her favorite episode was the special 4th of July episode the shot. "It was so great – it was a family affair, for sure. To have everyone there to celebrate – it's such a special memory!"

Sue loved having the kids on the show with us. "Teaching them to eat better will offset the problems of obesity that Jen and I suffered from. I know that I learned to cook by the age of 7 and by 12, I was baking and making a full meal for my folks who both worked." In her own childhood, she says, "We raised a garden and had all the fresh vegetables and fruit available during the spring, summer and fall." She loves helping to pass on more healthy traditions to her grandchildren. Her favorite recipes this season were the stews, soups, and chillis. "I loved taking old standard favorites and giving them a twist.

One of our favorite moments of this season was catching Jen's husband, Ronnie, snitching food off the counter during one of the episodes. Sue says, "I love it when the guys are caught up in the aroma and their mouths are watering!"

From Be My Valentine

Sue's Flourless Chocolate Cake

12 Bariatric Servings (1 cupcake or 2 mini cupcakes per serving)

1 pound bittersweet chocolate, chopped into small pieces (boxes of baking chocolate are 4 oz. each so you will need 4 boxes)
1 Stick unsalted butter
9 large eggs separated
¾ C stevia
1 tablespoon vanilla flavoring
dash salt

Preheat oven to 350 degrees F.

Grease cupcake pan or mini cupcake pan with butter or cooking spray. Make a double boiler by placing a bowl with the chopped chocolate and butter over a pan with gently simmering water. Mix with a spatula until completely melted and smooth. Beat the 9 egg yolks with the ¾ cup of stevia until the mixture is a light yellow. Beat the 9 egg whites in a separate bowl until strong peaks are formed. Temper the eggs by adding small amounts of the warm chocolate butter mixture into the egg yolk mixture until the two mixtures are combined. The chocolate and eggs will become stiff so don't be concerned.

Start adding ⅓ of the Egg White mixture into the chocolate mixture and FOLD GENTLY - try not to flatten the egg white mixture!!
When completely mixed, divide into the prepared baking cups

(A 9 inch spring form pan may be substituted for the baking cups but to maintain portion control we strongly suggest the baking cups)

Set the oven timer for 8 minutes, then half way through check the cakes with a toothpick the pick should come out with some of the batter in flakes on it. If you cook the full eight minutes and it is still runny, check every 2-3 minutes. These cook fast in the baking cups.

Serve with whipped cream or use a sugar free sauce like chocolate or caramel sauce to drizzle the top of the cake. These taste better if warmed in the microwave for 10-15 seconds.

Jen's Stuffed Portobello for Two

2 Bariatric Servings (1/2 mushroom per serving)

1 Portobello cap, stem removed and wiped clean with a moist towel
1/2 block cream cheese
1/4 C parmesan cheese
1/4 C mozzarella cheese
1 clove garlic
2 T chopped fresh herbs (I used basil)
salt and pepper to taste

Preheat oven to 425.

In a mixing bowl combine cream cheese, cheeses, herbs, garlic, and salt and pepper until well combined. Mound into the mushroom cap. Place in baking dish and bake for 15-20 minutes or until cheese is melty and slightly browned on top. Allow to come to room temperature before eating to allow center to "settle" and firm up!

Sue's Venison in Blackberry Sauce

2-3 Bariatric Servings (2-3 oz. per serving)

6 oz. venison fillet or two 3 oz. venison fillet (you can also use beef)
Marinade
½ C Wine of your choice
½ C of Vegetable Oil
2 C Garlic
½ small onion, chopped
1 Tablespoon Worcestershire Sauce

Add venison to Marinade leave at least 2 hours, overnight is even better! Grill for 2 - 3 minutes on each side. Serve rare for best flavor

BlackBerry Sauce

1 C Blackberries
2 -3 T butter
1 C blackberry wine (or red or white wine)
½ squeezed lemon
pepper / salt to taste

Combine all ingredients in a saucepan. Bring to a boil over medium-medium high heat. Reduce heat to low and simmer for 10-15 minutes, or until reduced. Strain sauce if desired.

Jen's Shrimp Hearts with Lemon Garlic marinade

2 servings (2-3 shrimp per serving)

Marinade:
Juice of 1 lemon
2 garlic cloves
1-2 T fresh chopped tarragon
1/4 C olive oil
salt and pepper to taste

Heat an indoor grill over high heat (or use an outdoor grill if you prefer, just be sure to use metal skewers or to soak your wooden ones for 20-30 minutes first).

Combine marinade ingredients in a bowl. Pour about half into a shallow dish.

Dip shrimp into the marinade and place on skewers in alternating directions so they form a heart shape. Put onto grill pan and cook 2-3 minutes per side or until opaque and cooked through (close the lid on an indoor grill for even faster cooking!) Brush some of the reserved marinade over the cooked shrimp for a flavor boost!

From Holding On To Winter: Recipes to Warm Your Soul!

Mama's No-Roux Gumbo

24 Bariatric Servings (1/2 C per serving)

2 T olive oil
2 T butter
2 medium onions, chopped finely (about 2 cups)
1 C bell pepper chopped finely
½ C celery chopped finely
2 cloves garlic chopped finely
2 C white wine
2 qt. or more of chicken broth or stock
1 lb. good smoked sausages
1 ½ C of shredded chicken
1 lb. of shrimp
1 lb. of unbreaded frozen okra
2 T Worcestershire Sauce
2-3 tsp. of Cajun seasoning, we use mild
1 ½ T of Louisiana style hot sauce (to your taste)
1 large can of diced tomatoes

In a large pot, brown the vegetables in the olive oil and butter until translucent. Add wine and seasonings. Add okra, sausage and shredded chicken. Bring to a strong boil for about 15-20 minutes. Check to make sure the okra is beginning to soften. Add the cleaned shrimp just about 5 minutes before serving.

Jen's Crock-Pot French Onion Soup

24 Bariatric Servings (1/2 C per serving)

3-4 onions (whichever kind you like best)
2 cloves minced garlic
3-4 sprigs thyme
1 box beef stock or 4 cups homemade
1 cup red wine
salt and pepper to taste
2 T butter
2 T olive oil or coconut oil

Sauté onions in butter over medium-low heat until caramelized (will take about 20 minutes - be sure to stir them often!). This can be done in advance and the onions stored in a container in the fridge for up to two days. Toss them into the crock pot with the thyme, stock, and salt and pepper. Turn crock pot on low heat and cook for up to 8 hours. Ladle into soup bowls and top with shredded cheese of choice (we used Jarlsburg Swiss). Stick under the broiler for a few minutes until cheese is melted and browned.

Individual Zucchini Lasagna

1 Bariatric Serving (with leftovers)

½ zucchini, sliced into thin rounds
½ C cooked and crumbled Italian sausage
1/2 C ricotta cheese
1 egg
2 T Parmesan
1/4 C mozzarella or other cheese
a few leaves of basil, torn
salt and pepper to taste

Get a small (1/2 C size) ramekin (we found ours at a mega mart for around a dollar!) and grease it in whatever manner you choose (butter, cooking spray, coconut oil ...). Put a tablespoon of sauce on the bottom. Place a few rounds of zucchini on top of the sauce (it's okay to overlap a little), put a spoonful of ricotta mix on top of the zucchini, then a spoonful of sausage. Add a bit of sauce and a tiny sprinkle of cheese, then top with more zucchini. Repeat with more ricotta, sausage, sauce, and cheese. Top with another zucchini round and more sauce and cheese. Bake at 375 for 15-20 minutes, or until browned and bubbly.

This is a great recipe to make up several of and store them in the freezer. Alternatively, you can slice the zucchini lengthwise and do this as a full-batch in a big ol' pan! If you do the bigger pan, however, you will need to lengthen the cooking time to about 30-45 minutes.

From Spring Has Sprung

Jen's Shrimp Sauté

1-2 Bariatric Servings (about 4 shrimp and ½ C veggies)

4-5 stalks asparagus, trimmed and cut into 1-in pieces
3-4 cherry tomatoes, sliced
2-3 artichoke hearts, cut into bite-size pieces (feel free to trim off the leaves!)
1 tsp. minced garlic
juice of 1/2 lemon
handful shrimp, cleaned (remove the tails or don't – it's personal preference!)

Heat a pan over medium heat. Melt in about a tablespoon of butter and a little olive or coconut oil. Toss in the veggies and sauté for a few minutes. Add the shrimp and garlic and continue to sauté until shrimp are done (they will turn pink and opaque, and curl up a bit). Add the lemon and toss. Turn off the heat and serve!

From *St. Patrick's Day Fun*

Jen's Gluten Free Chocolate Cupcakes

24 Bariatric Servings (1 cupcake per serving)

1 Package gluten-free chocolate cake mix
2 eggs
1/4 C stevia
2 tsp. vanilla
1 can no-sugar-added root beer (we like the ones that are made with stevia!)
1/2 C butter, softened

Put butter into mixer and mix it until it's fluffy and light. Add the eggs, vanilla and stevia and mix until well blended. Add the cake mix and root beer and mix on low 30 seconds or until just blended then raise the speed to high and beat for 2 minutes more or until light and fluffy. Use a cookie scoop to transfer the mix to mini-muffin tins. Bake at 350 for 15-20 minutes or until a toothpick comes clean when inserted into the center. Allow to cool in pan for a few minutes then transfer to a wire cooling rack to finish cooling completely before icing with frosting of choice.

Sue's Chocolate Guinness Cupcakes

24 Bariatric Servings (1 cupcake per serving)

1 Box Sugar Free Cake Mix
1 Can Guinness Irish stout beer

Combine all ingredients in bowl, mixing well. Using an ice cream scoop or 2/3 C measure, measure the mixture into lined cupcake tins. Bake at 325 for 20-25 minutes, or until a toothpick comes out clean when inserted into the middle of a cupcake. Allow to cool for 5 minutes in tins, then remove and complete cooling on a cooling rack before icing.

Semi-Famous Cream Cheese Icing

2 blocks cream cheese, softened
1/4-1/2 C sugar substitute (we like stevia)
2 tsp. vanilla
1 T heavy cream

Put cream cheese into mixer bowl and add vanilla and 1/4 C of the sugar substitute. Mix until almost fluffy. Taste. If desired, add more sweetener. Add cream and mix until fluffy. Store in airtight container for up to 3 days.

Sue's Irish Stout Braised Beef Ribs

About 10-16 Bariatric Servings (2-3 oz. per serving)
2 lbs. Beef Short Ribs
2 onions, sliced
1 can Guinness or other Irish stout beer
1 box beef broth
Salt and Pepper to taste

Heat 2 tsp oil in a skillet and heat over high heat. Add ribs and brown on all sides.
Place ribs into crock pot and cover with onions.
Add beer and broth and seasonings.
Cook on low for up to 12 hours.
Remove from slow cooker onto serving platter and allow to rest for at least 10 minutes before serving.

From An Egg-cellent Episode

Sue's Green Chili Egg Casserole

12 bariatric servings (2 mini bites or 1 bite per serving)
9 eggs
2 C cheese – we used a mixture of cheddar and habanero jack cheese
3 small cans mild green chilis
1 T Louisiana hot sauce (optional)
1/4 tsp. cayenne pepper (optional)
1/2 tsp. each black pepper and salt

Mix all ingredients in large bowl.

For bites: transfer mixture by the 1/4 cupful into muffin tins or mini muffin tins (2 T per mini muffin tin, 1/4 C per regular size muffin tin). Bake at 350 for 10-15 minutes or until slightly browned and puffy. These WILL shrink when cooling! This is normal and is supposed to happen!

For full-size casserole: transfer mix into casserole dish. Bake at 350 for 30-35 minutes or until slightly browned and puffy.

For both versions: Allow these to cool for at least 10 minutes before eating!

How To Boil an Egg

Place 3-6 eggs into a saucepan and cover with water. Slowly bring to a boil over medium heat. Once they come to a rolling boil, cover and remove from the heat. Allow to sit for 15-20 minutes then run cold water over the eggs until they're cooled. Store in the fridge unpeeled for up to a week, or peel and store in the fridge in an air tight container for a couple of days.

From *Easter Made Easy*

Cornish Game Hens

Recipe is for 1 game hen
About 3-4 Bariatric servings (2-3 oz. per serving)

Preheat oven to 350
Prepare 1 game hen for every 2 people

Per game hen:

2 T butter, cut into small pats
2-3 tsp. fresh rosemary, chopped
Salt and pepper to taste

Rinse and pat dry the hen, then transfer to a baking sheet or roasting pan. Press butter into the rosemary and place pats under the skin. Take any remaining butter and rub over skin. Sprinkle skin with salt and pepper to taste. Tent with foil and roast at 350 for 25-30 minutes, then remove foil and continue roasting for an additional 25-30 minutes or until hen is done (meat thermometer will read around 160). Allow to rest for 15-20 minutes before serving.

From Good Fats

Jen's Avocado Salad with Shrimp

2 Bariatric Servings (1/2 recipe)

Dressing:
Juice of 1 large, 2 medium, or 4 small limes (should come out to be about 1/4-1/3 C lime juice)
2 T extra virgin olive oil
1 T low-sodium or salt free fajita seasoning
Salt and Pepper to Taste

Salad:
1 Avocado, diced (see the video for instructions!)
1/2 red onion, diced
handful cilantro, chopped
1/4 lb. shrimp, cooked (may chop if desired)

Combine dressing ingredients in a large bowl with a whisk until well incorporated. Add salad ingredients and toss to coat. Allow to sit in refrigerator for up to two hours to chill and marry the seasonings, if desired. Serve cold!

From <u>Beautiful Breakfast</u>

<u>Sue's Almond Flour "S'muffins"</u>

12 bariatric servings (2 mini muffins per serving)

2 ½ C blanched almond flour
½ tsp. sea salt
½ tsp. baking soda
⅓ C coconut oil
¼ C honey or agave nectar
2 large eggs
½ tsp. cinnamon or more if desired

Combine dry ingredients in a large bowl. Combine wet ingredients in a smaller bowl. Add the wet ingredients to the dry ingredients and mix gently but thoroughly. Add add-ins of choice (blueberries, nuts, chopped apples, bananas, chocolate chips, etc.) and stir to combine. Using a cookie scoop or tablespoon fill mini-muffin tins lined with paper liners (about 1 scoop or 2 tablespoons of batter per muffin).

Bake 15 to 18 minutes at 325 until done (they will be well browned and slightly firm to the touch).

options: 1 cup sugar free chocolate chips, 1 cup blueberries, 1 cup chopped apple, 1 cup chopped banana

From <u>Eat Your Veggies!</u>

<u>Chicken Fajita Rolls-Ups</u>

3 bariatric servings

1-9 oz. chicken breast scaloppini, pounded to 1/4 in thickness and cut into thirds
1 C sautéed sliced vegetables (we used onions and bell peppers)

Marinade:
Juice of 1 large or 3 smaller limes
1/4 C vinegar of choice (we used white wine vinegar)
1 T fajita seasoning

Combine all ingredients in shallow dish and immerse chicken into it. Allow to marinade for about 15 minutes, turning once halfway through. Don't worry if your chicken turns a little white – that is absolutely normal. It means the vinegar and lime juice are working!

Assembly:

Take 1/3 of a chicken breast, blot it with paper towels to dry and lay out in front of you lengthwise. Lay out a few slices of your veggies (about 1/3C) and roll it up. Place it seam side down on a greased baking sheet. Bake them at 375 for 15-20 minutes or until chicken is cooked through. Allow to rest for about 10 minutes before eating!

From 4th of July Special 2014

Jen's Super Sliders

16 bariatric servings

1 lb. Lean Ground Beef
1/4 C bottled steak sauce of choice
cheddar cheese that has been sliced into 1/4 in. thick slices and cut to slider size (optional)
slider buns or good soft rolls (optional)

Combine beef and steak sauce.
Using an ice cream scoop, portion out meat and flatten slightly into small patty size.
Grill over medium high heat 3-5 minutes per side (the meat will be ready to flip when it no longer sticks to the grill).

STUFFED SLIDERS OPTION:
Flatten out the patty and stick a piece of cheese in the middle. Bring the meat up and over the sides and smoosh and flatten until the cheese is covered. Grill according to above directions.

To serve:

Place a patty on a slider roll or lettuce leaf and top with favorite toppings! (Jen's favorites: Lettuce, pickle, and mayo!)

The Roadkill Seasoning

Jen and Sue both have their own versions of this recipe, and (for once) Sue's is LESS complicated than Jen's! Both are delicious, however, and really enhance the flavor of whatever savory dish you're making.

Sue's Version

1 C kosher salt
1/4 C black pepper
1/4 C garlic powder
1/4 C onion powder
2 T cayenne pepper

Jen's Version

1 C kosher salt
2 T black pepper
2 T garlic powder
2 T onion powder
2 tsp. thyme
2 tsp. ground mustard
2 tsp. paprika

For both versions: Toss ingredients into a jar and shake!

Sue's Mock-A-Roni Salad

8-16 Bariatric Servings (1/4 – ½ C)

1 head of Cauliflower
1 bell pepper of any color
1 C of black olives (we like Kalamata olives)
1 C of chopped pepperoni slices
2 green onions chop the whole onions
1 jar of marinated artichoke hearts
1 jar of pepperoncini
1 bottle of Italian dressing (we used an amazing balsamic vinaigrette from our local fruit stand!)

Chop the cauliflower into bite-sized pieces and boil in salted water until tender. Cool completely. Chop the bell pepper into small pieces, along with the olives, onions and artichoke hearts. Uniform pieces are better to mix evenly. Cut the pepperoni slices in half. We did not chop the Pepperoncini up because some of our family don't care for them and they look good whole. Pour ½ the vinaigrette over the mixture and stir to see if everything is coated. After it sets an hour you may want to add more. Chill for at least two hours, but even better when chilled overnight!

VEGETARIANS: Omit the pepperoni and away you go!

Sue's Bacon Wrapped Jalapeño Poppers

Number of servings depends on how many jalapeños are in the pint. 1 jalapeño = 1 serving

Cut slits in a pint of fresh jalapeños and remove as many seeds and as much of the membrane as possible. Set aside.

In a large bowl combine 2 blocks of softened cream cheese with 1 lb. shredded pepper jack (we found a great chipotle-cheddar that is AWESOME).

Gently stuff each pepper with a couple of tablespoons of mixture (stuff until it looks good to you!) and wrap each in a couple of pieces of bacon, using a toothpick that's been soaked in water for an hour or so to secure.

Grill over medium heat, turning frequently, until bacon is crisp and peppers are tender (about 10-15 minutes)

Cinnamon Ice Cream with Grilled Peaches

8-12 Bariatric Servings With leftover ice cream (1/2 peach and ¼ C ice cream)

Grilled Peaches

4 -6 ripe peaches
1 tsp. cinnamon

Cut in half and remove the pit. Sprinkle with cinnamon and place inside down on a hot grill, leave long enough to get distinct grill marks.

Cinnamon Ice-Cream

1 C Whole Milk
¾ C stevia
pinch salt
2 Cups Heavy Cream
2 tsp. cinnamon
1 T pure vanilla extract

In a medium bowl use a whisk to combine the milk, sweetener, salt and cinnamon until dissolved. Stir in the heavy cream and vanilla. Cover and refrigerated up to 2 hours or overnight.

We used an ice cream maker and followed the directions of the manufacturer. It took about 20-25 minutes for the ice cream to be soft-serve ready!

Note: this is a basic ice cream recipe and any flavoring can be added by substituting for the cinnamon.

Emily's Chicken Arms

5-8 Bariatric Servings (1-2 wings per serving)

1 lb. chicken wings
Juice of 3 large lemons
3-5 cloves garlic (depending on taste and size), minced
1/4 C olive oil
1 T roadkill seasoning

Combine all ingredients in plastic bag.

Prep the chicken "arms" (chicken wings) by cutting off the wing tip and separating the drumette from the wingette.

Put the chicken into the bag and seal. Either shake or massage the chicken, then allow to sit for up to an hour (flipping the bag once) to marinate.

Grill over medium heat for 5-6 minutes per side (chicken is ready to flip when it no longer sticks to the grill).

Season 3

Season 3 brought about a shift in thinking for 7 Bites. We began to think about the bariatric patient that was new to the kitchen. Many obese people have never cooked food from scratch and only relied on pre-packaged meals and fast food. We came up with the idea of "Bariatric 101" Episodes that explained how to cook simple and easy proteins to have on hand.

Jen remembers, "I could cook before surgery, but I literally had to re-learn everything. We really wanted to make this season about returning to the basics and teaching people that had never cooked before or who had to re-learn cooking for surgery." Her favorite episode of this season was "Thinking Outside the Box". "It was really a pivotal episode for me. I'd seriously never had anything with green chilis prior to filming, so to learn that I liked it opened up a lot of doors for me. I began trying things I'd never had before and became more adventurous in my cooking." That new confidence inspired her favorite recipe from this season, Low Carb Pumpkin Muffins. "I literally threw this recipe together in the kitchen one day on a whim. I'd never done that before, and it paid off!"

Sue loved being able to play with food more this season. She also enjoyed creating new and interesting ideas for batch cooking. "We learned that batch-cooking was and will always be a good method for people with our eating needs." Her favorite episode this season was the Halloween episode. "I always love dressing up and for Halloween we came up with the idea of the Blues Brothers. But nothing topped our first season with Paula Deen and Ree Drummond! Halloween is my favorite holiday, and I love making treats that are friendly to our tummies." She also enjoys doing episodes focused around questions and requests from viewers. "I like doing food demos showing folks how easy it can be to have a tasty meal in just a few minutes. I like to play with my food, even if I can only eat 7-10 bites!"

From _Yuck-in-a-Cup Redoux_

Jen's Protein Peach Smoothie

Protein drinks don't have to be scary anymore! Jen adds peaches to this one. Using the vanilla chai flavored powder gives the mix a little bit of a peach cobbler flavor. If using plain vanilla powder, try adding a dash of cinnamon!

1 Bariatric Serving

1 serving protein powder of choice, prepared according to package directions (we used Vanilla Chai vegan powder prepared with almond milk)
1/2 peach

Puree peach in blender or personal blender. Add protein drink and blend until smooth. Serve in chilled glass.

Also works well with vanilla protein powder. If you chose to use unflavored, we recommend adding 1/4 tsp vanilla and a bit of sweetener

If you are on the full liquids stage, be sure to strain into the glass!!

Sue's Protein Blueberry Smoothie

1 Bariatric Serving

Protein drinks and smoothies don't have to be scary! In this version, Sue gives it a blueberry pie flavor using real blueberries and ups the protein by adding Greek yogurt. This is a thicker shake and a little more savory. If desired, add some sweetener to the mix.

1 serving protein powder of choice (we used a vanilla egg white protein)
8 oz. coconut milk
2 T (1/8 C) Greek yogurt
Handful fresh or frozen blueberries
a few ice cubes

Put everything into a personal blender cup and blend for a few seconds until ice is broken up and everything is well blended. Pour into serving glass and enjoy.

For those on full liquids, be sure to strain this first!

From More Protein Power

Protein Donuts with Cream Cheese Icing

12 Bariatric Servings (1 Donut or 2 mini muffins per serving)

1/2 C Unflavored Protein Powder + 1/2 C Sugar Substitute (OR 1/2 C Vanilla Protein Powder + 1/4 C Sugar Substitute)
1/2 C Gluten Free Baking Mix
1 C ground almond meal
1 tsp. baking powder
2 tsp. cinnamon
1/4 tsp. salt
1 egg
no-sugar-added pie filling (we used cherry)
1 tsp. vanilla

Pre-heat oven to 325

Directions:
Mix all ingredients in a bowl until well combined.
Spoon into donut pan or mini-muffin tin.
Bake.
Muffin Bites: 10-12 minutes
Donuts: 12-15 minutes

Check after 10 minutes, inserting a toothpick or knife into the donut/bites. If it comes out clean, they are done. If there is batter on it, leave another few minutes.

Icing:
1 package cream cheese, softened
1/2 C sucralose or stevia
1 tsp. vanilla
splash heavy cream or milk to thin a bit

Mix all ingredients with hand mixer or in standing mixer until well combined. If needed, add more sweetener to taste or more liquid too thin to get the flavor and consistency you desire.

From <u>Thinking Outside the Box</u>

Green Chili Chicken Stew

24 Bariatric Servings (1/2 C per serving)

1 small chicken, boiled or roasted, skin removed, and shredded
1 onion, chopped
1 green bell pepper, chopped
1 can green chilis
1 can green chili enchilada sauce
1 can white beans of choice UNDRAINED
2 C chicken stock
salt and pepper to taste
olive oil, coconut oil, or butter for sautéing

In a heavy bottomed soup pot, heat a tablespoon of olive oil over medium heat. Add onions and bell peppers and sautee until tender, adding salt and pepper to taste. Add garlic and cook for another minute or two. Add remaining ingredients and stir gently to combine. Bring to a boil. Reduce heat to medium low and simmer 15-20 minutes. Allow to rest for about 10 minutes to thicken.

NOTE for those on full liquids or purees, run this through the blender!

Serving suggestion: top with Greek yogurt or sour cream and some cheese!

From Keep It Simple

Mexican Shrimp Cocktail

Full Recipe:
4-6 ½ C servings

1 pound shrimp – any size
1 quart of tomato juice with clam juice already infused
1 8 oz. package of Pico de Gallo
1 avocado chopped in large chunks
1 lemon or lime juiced

Single Serve Recipe:
6-8 Shrimp
1 C tomato juice with clam juice already infused
2 T packaged Pico de Gallo
1 T chopped avocado
1 T lemon or lime juice

Bring 2-3 quarts of water to a boil then add crab/seafood boil seasoning to the pan. Drop in the boiling water for 2-3 minutes tops. When the shrimp start to turn pink drain them immediately.

Put the drained shrimp in a large measuring cup, pour the tomato drink over the shrimp, mix in 2-3 tablespoons (heaping) Pico de Gallo, the chopped avocado, and lemon/lime juice to taste.

Let stand in the refrigerator until shrimp are completely cooled. If you use purchased precooked shrimp make sure they are thawed before serving the cocktail.

Stuffed Squash

Side Dish: 6 Bariatric Servings (1/2 Squash)
Main Dish: 3 Bariatric Servings (1 Squash)

Filling:
1 block cream cheese, softened
1 c cheddar cheese
3 small yellow squash, halved
cooked bacon (optional – omit it to keep it vegetarian!)

Crumble bacon into cream cheese and add cheese. Mix until well combined.
Spread mixture onto squash halves.
Bake at 375 until hot, bubbly, and browned.
Allow to rest for a few minutes before eating.

From Bariatric Cooking 101: Simple Staples

Bariatric Scrambled Eggs (Soft-Foods Eggs)

1 Bariatric Serving

1 egg
2 tsp. heavy cream, half and half, milk, or water
1 T butter or oil
salt and pepper to taste

Heat oil or butter in a pan over medium heat until melted. Meanwhile, crack an egg into a bowl and add your liquid. Using a fork or whisk, beat the egg until well combined. Add egg to pan and begin to stir immediately using a silicone spatula or a wooden spoon. Continue stirring over medium heat until the egg is slightly glistening and custard-like. Add salt and pepper to taste and remove from heat. Don't worry if the egg doesn't look completely cooked at first, it will continue to cook slightly after you remove it from the heat. Serve warm.

How To Boil Shrimp

Number of servings depends on how many shrimp are in the pound. 1 Serving = 4-6 shrimp

1 lb. Shrimp (we used jumbo sized easy-peal shrimp)
2 T Shrimp Boil (you can also use whatever seafood seasoning you like)
2 qt. water (enough to cover shrimp)

Bring water to a boil. Add shrimp boil or seafood seasoning. Gently add shrimp. Boil until shrimp are pink, opaque, and just slightly curled (remember they will continue cooking slightly when removed from the water) – about 5 minutes. Remove from heat and drain. Serve immediately or chill.

Potato-Leek Soup with Bacon

24 Bariatric Servings (1/2 C)

8 medium potatoes about 1 – 1 ½ pounds
2 leeks – cut into pieces
1- 12-16 oz. package of smoked bacon
1 (2 C) pt. whole cream
1- 32 oz. box of chicken broth or stock
½ pound of good cheddar cheese (I used New York Cheddar)
Salt and pepper to taste

Peel and cup potatoes into dice, place in a large saucepan and cover with broth or stock. (make sure you just cover the potatoes you will not be draining the potatoes)

Cut the leeks lengthwise then chop into bite size pieces. Place the leeks into a large bowl filled with cold water and swish around to help remove sand that may be hidden in the layers of leek. Allow the sand to settle to the bottom of the bowl then lift the leeks out and allow to drain in a strainer.

Sauté the bacon in a large skillet. When the bacon is browned remove from the bacon drippings and allow to drain on a paper towel. Place the drained leeks into the bacon drippings and sauté until tender, set aside.

When the potatoes are fork tender add the leeks to the potatoes and broth allow to continue to simmer. Chop the bacon into small bites size pieces. Add it to the potato leek mixture continuing to simmer. Measure the cream adding it slowly to the potato leek mixture.

Grate the cheddar cheese and mix into the soup letting it melt before serving.

To serve as a pureed or full liquids meal, transfer soup by the cupful into a personal blender, blender, or food processor. Pulse to puree. Transfer to 1/2 C sized storage containers to freeze.

From Peachy Keen!

Peach Pie Bites

12 bariatric Servings (1 bite per serving)

1 Large peach, peeled and chopped
1 lemon – juiced
1 C peach butter
1 package puffed pastry
1 egg for egg wash

Thaw the puffed pastry, dust the board with flour, roll out the puffed pastry out till it is thin. Cut each sheet of pastry into thirds. Use the seams as your guide.

Mix lemon juice with chopped peaches. Add the peach butter to the mixture of apples and lemon.

Place about a teaspoon of mixture on to the pastry.

Stretch the second strip of pastry over the first and seal as if it is ravioli. Then cut into pieces and press the edges with a fork to crimp to seal.

Beat the egg in a bowl with 3 tablespoons of water, spread over the pie pieces, this will make the pie pieces brown evenly.

Spray a baking sheet with cooking spray place the pieces about 1 inch apart on the pan. Set the oven at 425 degrees. Cook for 12-15 minutes on center shelf of the oven. Oven temperatures may vary so watch them closely the last 5 minutes.

From <u>Pizza Party</u>

<u>Bariatric Friendly Pizza – Three Ways!</u>

For many of us, pizza is one thing that is missed above many other foods. But it doesn't have to be! We've found three ways to make pizza in smaller portions, using bariatric-friendly ingredients.

Pizza 1: Use a whole wheat or carb-friendly tortilla for a crust. Spread with pizza sauce or other favorite sauce and top with your favorite pizza toppings.

Pizza 2: Use 1/2 a whole wheat or carb-friendly English muffin for a crust. Spread with pizza sauce or other favorite sauce and top with your favorite pizza toppings.

Pizza 3: At your local deli counter, ask for some thick sliced pepperoni. Use the slices of pepperoni as your crust and spread with pizza sauce or other favorite sauce. Top with your favorite pizza toppings.

Some of our favorite pizza toppings:
Pepperoni, mushrooms, olives, chopped onion, chopped bell pepper, cooked and crumbled Italian sausage, ham or Canadian bacon, pineapple, cooked and crumbled hamburger.

Don't like pizza sauce? Use Alfredo sauce instead!

Meat-za Bites

12 Bariatric Servings (2 bites per serving)

1/2 lb. Italian sausage
1/2 lb. lean ground beef
1/2 C chopped pepperoni
1 C jarred pizza or spaghetti sauce (or use your favorite) plus 1/2 C (reserve to the side)
2 T chopped onion
2 T chopped bell pepper
1/2 C shredded mozzarella cheese
2 eggs, slightly beaten

Combine meats, pizza sauce, onion, bell pepper, and eggs in a large bowl. Mix well with hands to combine. Use a cookie scoop to transfer to mini muffin tins. Top each bite with a tsp. of sauce and a sprinkle of cheese. Bake at 375 for 15-20 minutes, or until center reaches 160 degrees.

From Bariatric Cooking 101: Storing Portions

Chicken Lasagna Roll-Up

6-9 Bariatric Servings (2-3 oz. per serving)

Two 9 oz. Boneless Skinless chicken breasts, cut in half lengthwise and flattened (scallopenied)
Sliced provolone cheese
Shredded parmesan cheese (about 1/2 Cup)
Shredded mozzarella cheese (about 1/2 Cup)
1 C ricotta cheese flavored with extra parmesan, Italian seasoning, and salt and pepper to taste
Favorite tomato sauce
Extra mozzarella cheese for topping

Pre-Heat oven to 375

Flatten chicken breasts using a kitchen mallet or have your butcher flatten them for you. Lay flattened chicken breast out on clean cutting board and cut in half to portion.
Fill one have with 1/4 C ricotta cheese mixture and sprinkle with shredded parmesan and mozzarella.
Gently roll up and place seam side down in a greased baking pan. Repeat with remaining chicken and cheese.
Top with favorite tomato sauce and more cheese.
Bake at 375 for 20-25 minutes or until cheese is bubbling and browned.
Allow to rest for 10-15 minutes to cool and set before eating.

To freeze: Allow to cool completely in refrigerator. Remove each portion and place in storage container or plastic bag, making sure air is removed (these work beautifully with a vacuum sealer!). Freeze for up to 6 months.

To reheat:
Method 1: Allow to thaw in refrigerator. Remove from storage container or bag and place on baking pan. Cover with foil and bake at 350 for 15-20 minutes, or until heated through.
Method 2 (for use with vacuum sealer only): bring a large pot of water to boil. Place entire vacuum seal package into boiling water. Boil for 10-15 minutes or until heated through.

From *Happy Halloween*

Low-Carb Pumpkin Muffins with Homemade Whipped Cream

12 Bariatric Servings (2 mini muffins per serving)

Ingredients:
1 can pumpkin puree (NOT pumpkin pie filling!)
3 eggs
2 T peanut butter or other nut butter
1 1/2 C almond flour
1 tsp. baking powder
1 tsp. baking soda
1/4 tsp. salt
1 tsp. cinnamon
1 1/2 tsp. pumpkin pie spice
1/4 C sucralose or other sweetener

Line mini muffin tin with liners.
Combine all ingredients in a bowl. Mix until well combined and smooth (you may use a hand mixer or standing mixer, if desired).
Using a cookie scoop, transfer batter to muffin tins.
Bake at 350 for 15-20 minutes or until toothpick inserted into muffin comes out clean.

To cool: turn out onto clean dish towel and turn right-side up to cool to prevent soggy bottoms on your muffins.

From *Celebration Survival*

Pudding Parfait

1 Bariatric Serving

Ingredients:

1 single serving container pudding
1/4 C whipped cream
nuts, fruits, or other mix-ins of choice

Layer a spoonful of pudding into the bottom of a pretty glass. Top with mix ins. Top with whipped cream. Repeat. Consume. Smile.

From *Bariatric Cooking 101: Let's Do Lunch*

Retribution Stew

24 Bariatric Servings (1/2 C per serving)

2 lbs. of lean stew meat – we use venison but beef or lamb work just as well
1 Parsnip chopped roughly
1 medium sweet potato chopped roughly
1 leek
1 box (32 ounces) of Beef Broth

Cut the leek long wise then chopped into small bits, place in a large bowl of water and swish around let the leek pieces float to the top and dip them off to keep all the sand in the water.

Heat a skillet on medium high heat till piping hot.

Dredge the cubed stew meat in flour (all purpose or soy). Place the meat in the skillet watching it so that it only sears, remove pieces to a dish to hold. Doing these pieces in batches makes the browning go much faster.

Place all the ingredients into the crockpot, put the meat on the bottom as it takes the longest to cook, cover everything with the broth. (This can be cooked on top of the stove instead of the crockpot but you have to be very attentive to make sure it doesn't stick.)

Crock pots vary but a rule of thumb is low for 8-10 hours, high for 4-6 hours. Cooking on top of the stove requires that the mixture is brought to a boil then reduced to a simmer for about 1 ½ hours. Check it often to make sure there is enough broth.

From <u>Bariatric Friendly Thanksgiving</u>!

Turkey Rollups

10 Bariatric Servings

5 to 10 - ¼ inch thick Deli Turkey

** I used Mesquite Smoked but there are lots of flavors to choose from. This amount of turkey can be reduced as 10 pieces will feed a lot of people and 5 cut in half after stuffing will be 10 portions. So figure out how much you need before you start.

1 package precooked quinoa (8 oz.)
½ tart apple cubed
½ pear cubed
Salt and Pepper to taste
¼ tsp. thyme (optional)
¼ tsp. Marjoram (optional)

This is one mixture you can taste as you season to make sure it has enough herbs and salt.

Set oven at 350 degrees and bake for 20 minutes until fruit is tender.

Pumpkin Pie Bites in Filo Cups

12-24 Bariatric Servings (1-2 Bites per serving)

Heat oven to 350 degrees.

1 Box of uncooked filo dough thawed (takes about 1 hour)
½ stick of butter melted
1 pastry brush

Filling
¾ C stevia
½ tsp. salt
1 ¾ tsp. Pumpkin Pie Spice
2 large eggs (beaten)
1 can (15 oz.) pureed pumpkin
1 can (12 oz.) evaporated milk (low fat can be used)

This is a process so don't get in a hurry!

Mix all the ingredients for the filling in a large bowl until smooth.

Unroll the filo dough. It is in layers. Gently pull apart about 3 layers of the dough, one at a time, coating it with the melted butter.
Lay the next layer on top of the buttered layer. Now fold all three layers over making six layers. Cut into pieces that will fit into a mini muffin tin. This may be about 2 X 2 squares, try one then

adjust. The dough will overhang the top of the tin. You may trim the edges but it is totally unnecessary. Just make sure that the dough in pushed into the tin and is reasonably smooth. I often spray the tin with cooking spray so that it will slide around and get smooth, but it is not necessary for the cups to pop out of the tin.

Now fill each tin with the filling mixture. This should be enough filling for 48 mini cup bites.

Alternatively, you may purchase pre-made filo cups in the freezer section of your local supermarket. It will be near the pie crusts and whipped topping.

Bake the mini cups 25 minutes. Bake the Mini Tart cups for 35 minutes. Remember ovens may vary so be attentive the last 5 minutes. The filling should be firm and tender, not hard.

From Freezer Pull

Chicken Mock-Ito's

6 Bariatric Servings (2 mock-ito's per serving)

1 Can red enchilada sauce
2 C shredded chicken (we used a rotisserie chicken)
2 C shredded cheddar cheese. divided
12 slices deli chicken

Pour ½ the sauce in a baking pan. Lay a slice of chicken on the counter and fill with shredded chicken and about a tablespoon of cheese. Place seam side down in a baking pan. Repeat with remaining ingredients. Cover with remaining sauce and the remaining cheese.

From <u>Pot Luck Perfection</u>

<u>Taco Soup</u>

24 Bariatric Servings (1/2 C per serving)

2 T olive oil
1 lb. lean ground beef
1 can black beans, drained
1 C frozen corn (optional)
1 onion, chopped
1 bell pepper, chopped (any color)
1 T minced garlic OR 3 garlic cloves, minced
1 packet low-sodium taco seasoning
4 C water OR beef broth OR chicken broth

Sauté peppers and onion in 2 T olive oil until tender. Add garlic and beef and cook until meat is almost cooked. Add broth and taco seasoning. Bring to a boil over medium high heat. Reduce heat to low and simmer for 15-20 minutes. Add corn and simmer for another 5 minutes. Add beans and continue to simmer for another 5 minutes. Serve warm topped with cheese if desired.

A Final Word

We love feeding family and friends and all the recipes we use have been taste tested on our Guinea Pigs (also known as our family). We only put the ones that pass the taste test on our show. We try to make our recipes as easy and quick to throw together as possible. We also try to make recipes that are not so large that a single person would be stuck with leftovers for months.

We hope you enjoyed cooking with us! If you have any requests or ideas for recipes, feel free to contact us! Remember you can always contact us via email, on Facebook, on our Facebook group, and on our website. We love to hear from our friends and would love to answer any questions you might have!

Remember you can contact us via email at SevenBitesShow@gmail.com, on Facebook at www.facebook.com/7Bites, on our Facebook group at www.facebook.com/groups/7Bites and on our website www.7Bites.net

And you can always visit us on our YouTube channel www.youtube.com/SevenBitesShow to Come See What We're Up To!

Printed in Great Britain
by Amazon